LifeLines

What You Absolutely, Positively Need To Know About Life!

by

Sharon Silver

dp

DISTINCTIVE PUBLISHING

LifeLines

Copyright © 1994 by Sharon Silver

Library of Congress Cataloging-in-Publication Data
Silver, Sharon, 1955 —
    LifeLines: What You Absolutely, Positively
    Need To Know About Life! / by Sharon Silver
        p.   cm.
    ISBN 0-942963-55-5 : $5.95
    1. Conduct of life   I. Title
BJ1581.2.S516 1994
170'.44—dc20   94-36735
                                                    CIP

Cover design by Chris Pearl
Interior design by Mary Bredbenner

Distinctive books are available at special discounts when purchased in bulk for premiums and sales promotions as well as for fund-raising or educational use. Special Editions or book excerpts can also be created to specification. For details, contact the Special Sales Director at the address below.

dp

DISTINCTIVE PUBLISHING CORP.
P.O. Box 17868
Plantation, Florida 33318-7868

Manufactured in the United States of America

Dedication

To my parents, who gave me life —
then taught me how to live.

Acknowledgments

For their invaluable contributions to **LifeLines**, I would like to thank Richard Westlund, my longtime editor; Robert Schimmel, whose expertise goes far beyond the scope of the law; and Geri Schimmel, my best friend and colleague.

Introduction

Throughout my life, I've been a collector of **LifeLines**. Family, friends and clients have contributed thousands of ideas, suggestions and insights over the years — helping me to develop my own highly practical philosophy of life.

LifeLines offers you the best of that accumulated wisdom — the secrets of successful living, meaningful relationships and inner happiness — and how to apply these often-forgotten concepts to the puzzles of contemporary life. Used properly, the knowledge contained in **LifeLines** will help you survive and thrive in today's fast paced society.

Like a good reference book, **LifeLines** will be there when you need it. Read each page at your own leisure, and profit from these suggestions.

— *Sharon Silver*

Hold or fold?

Successful people, like winning gamblers, know when to hold 'em and when to fold 'em. Sometimes a temporary setback can lead to long-term success. Look over opportunities as they present themselves, then decide whether you're holding a winning hand or whether to wait for the next deal. In the game of life, you hold all the cards.

The best job

When you feel overworked and underpaid, the best job always seems to belong to someone else. Doctors want to be lawyers and stockbrokers want to be shopkeepers. Managers want to be consultants and teachers want to be gardeners. Usually, when you feel this way, it's best to let the moment pass. The truth is that the grass is often greenest right where you stand.

Do it today

A famous author planned to write a book on "The Joy of Procrastination" — but he never got around to it. Too many people have great ideas and great plans, but they put off taking action. Don't make the same mistake. Whatever your goals, start now. Each day is a gift, so use it wisely.

Agree to disagree

You're a Democrat. Your friend is a Republican. Will that spoil your friendship? Not if you're smart. Why bicker with each other, when you can simply agree to disagree. Two healthy individuals will have no problem with that concept. After all, as the French say, "vive la difference!"

A bargain

. . . isn't always a bargain. When a store advertises the "sale of the century," you rush in and frantically fill your shopping cart. There are so many bargains, you can't resist. But before you get to the checkout counter, remember that just because you want something, that doesn't mean you need it!

Waist not

. . . want not. Many people are always fighting the battle of the bulge. But if you want to improve your height/weight ratio, there is a simple solution. Try eating just half the food on your plate. A little waste is a small price to pay for a little waist!

Cats and dogs

. . . make wonderful house pets, but dreadful bed mates. Fighting, kicking and scratching are poor ways to settle an argument. If you're angry, try taking a cold shower or walking around the block until you calm down. Do whatever it takes to blow off steam. But don't act like an animal, unless you enjoy spending time in the doghouse.

Customer loyalty

. . . has its perks. If you become a regular customer at the dry cleaner, hair stylist or butcher shop, you generally get better service. You become a person, not just a face with a purse or wallet. Companies know that their profitability is built on a base of loyal customers. Patronize the same stores and they will value your business.

LIFE

Don't be so busy making choices
that you forget to live.

— ◆ —

It's all right to wish for a miracle
— just don't rely on one.

— ◆ —

Life is a gift — how you use it
is up to you.

— ◆ —

Write your own script and be the
director of your life.

— ◆ —

If you invite trouble,
it always accepts.

— ◆ —

Live and let live.

A good night's sleep

If you suffer from insomnia, it's time to change your sleeping habits. Start establishing bedtime rituals. Do the same thing in the same order each night before bed, even on weekends. A tape of lullabies or soothing music can help relax you. Getting a good night's sleep doesn't have to be just a daydream.

Changing the world

. . . starts in your neighborhood. Instead of complaining about world issues, try planting a tree, picking up some trash or organizing a community crime-watch. You may be powerless to change events in Washington, London or Tokyo, but you have the clout to make a difference in your hometown. As more people take action, the world will become a better place to live.

The source of happiness

A century ago, after months of trekking, explorers discovered the source of the mysterious Nile. Fortunately, you don't have to travel thousands of miles to find the source of happiness — just look within. Happiness is a state of mind, and it is within reach of everyone. It's that person staring back at you in the mirror each morning who can make you happy — no one else.

Making a list

There are many advantages to making lists:

1. Lists help you keep track of your short-term and long-range goals.
2. Lists make it easy to measure how far you've come toward achieving your goals.
3. Writing things down will help keep you focused.
4. Lists free up your memory for more important tasks.

Give an important project to a list-maker — it's the best way to ensure it will be completed.

Married or single

To wed or not to wed — that really isn't the question. Today's single may be tomorrow's married, or vice versa. It doesn't matter which you choose, as long as you are happy with your choice. If getting married is high on your agenda, then be open to finding a mate. If you want to stay single, no one can force you to walk down the aisle. Your life can be a ringing success, with or without that band of gold.

Self defense

. . . begins with common sense. All the martial arts classes in the world won't replace good common sense. For your personal safety, be aware of your immediate surroundings and avoid potentially dangerous situations. There is never a right time to be in the wrong place.

Don't overdo

. . . whatever you do! In our goal-oriented society, everyone faces continuous pressure to do more — more at work, at play and at home. Pushing yourself to the limit can be hazardous to your physical and emotional health. Moderation is one of the secrets of life.

Accessories

. . . allow you to put your signature on what you wear. If you wear attention-getting jewelry, scarfs, ties or hats, no one will care whose name is on the label of your jacket. Personalizing your wardrobe helps you stand out from the crowd. The right pin, watch or cuff links can also add an element of class. Let your fashion accessories make a positive statement about your style.

ROMANCE

Boredom is one of the deadliest
enemies of romance.

— ◆ —

Savor the moment.

— ◆ —

Romantics see the world in
vivid color.

— ◆ —

If everything in love stayed the
same, intimacy would die.

— ◆ —

The best lovers are romantics.

— ◆ —

When it comes to romance, it's the
little things that count the most.

An expert

. . . is someone from out of town. People listen attentively when an "expert" arrives to solve a particular problem. You may have the same expertise, but everyone in your home town probably takes you for granted. A visiting expert has learned one of life's most important lessons — to be taken seriously, take a plane trip!

Send a surprise

Why wait for Valentine's Day to send roses, or a birthday to send a card? There are 365 opportunities every year to make someone feel special. An unsolicited gift, a thoughtful note or an unexpected bouquet will be appreciated. What a wonderful way to brighten a gloomy day.

No road

. . . is without detours. The same holds true in life. No matter what direction you go, there will always be twists, turns and curves. Only the inexperienced expect to travel in a straight line. When detours occur, just keep your eyes on the road, watch out for potholes and enjoy the ride!

$F_{ax\ it}$

The pace of life keeps increasing minute by minute. Why wait for the mail or a messenger when you can fax that important document. If something needs immediate attention, send a fax — and keep the transmittal sheet so you can verify a correspondence was sent. The fax machine is always a time saver. Sometimes, in the business world it can be a life saver as well.

Wet and wild

. . . can be a dangerous combination. Thousands of people drown every year in oceans, lakes, rivers and swimming pools. Many fatal accidents could have been prevented by taking precautions. Know how to swim and make sure children are always supervised around water. Enjoy the water — but treat it with respect!

Goof proof

Everyone makes mistakes, including you! When you goof up, admit it. Take responsibility for your error and try to correct it. That's one of the signs of maturity — trying to take a bad situation and make it better.

Jumping to conclusions

In a courtroom, a person is presumed innocent until proven guilty. Unfortunately, in many marriages a spouse is prosecuted and convicted long before the defense can present its case. If you're tempted to make snap judgments, collect all the facts before drawing a conclusion.

A creative outlet

The arts are for everyone. You don't need to be a famous painter, pianist or performer to enjoy the world of art, music, theater and dance. All you have to do is pick up a brush, guitar or ballet slippers. Many successful people cultivate a hobby in the arts. It's an excellent outlet for your creativity — and an excellent antidote to workaholism. Best of all, it's never too late to start!

A sixth sense

Five senses are not enough to live a happy life. Additionally, everyone needs a sense of humor! Jokes, pranks and jests add fun to the day-to-day routine. Being able to laugh at yourself is one of the best ways to relieve stress and tension. When you're feeling down, the best medicine is a strong dose of laughter.

EMOTIONS

Be sensitive, but know how and
when to show it.

Patience can't be bought by the
pound or sold by the ounce.

Being macho doesn't automatically
make you a man.

Remember the pain of the past to
avoid mistakes in the future.

Consult your heart and head before
making a decision.

Control your emotions in a crisis.

Home furnishings

. . . and decorations need to be chosen carefully. Professional decorators and friends can give their opinions, but you're the person who must live with the overstuffed sofa, the glass dining room table or the antique dresser. Try different combinations to see what appeals to you — then create a decor that suits your style and taste.

Overestimating

. . . is an excellent habit! In most social situations, it's better to overestimate than underestimate. Imagine how embarrassing it would be to run out of food at a wedding. On the financial side, wouldn't you rather retire with more money than not enough? Surplus creates peace of mind. Give yourself a cushion by overestimating.

Practice what you preach

It's easy to share your "pearls of wisdom" with others. Most people like to give advice and suggestions they feel will be beneficial. However, don't tell others to do something you're not willing to do yourself. If your motto is "Do as I say, not as I do," don't be surprised when people ignore your suggestions. Hypocrites can usually be spotted a mile away.

Take an interest

. . . in your partner's interests. When two people have nothing in common but each other, it's easy for problems to begin. Take time to gain an understanding and appreciation of your partner's interests. Sharing a recreational activity, hobby or leisure pursuit will go a long way toward strengthening a relationship. Couples that play together stay together.

Beware of the man

. . . who says he's not very bright. If someone tells you he's just "a good old country boy," watch out — he may be setting you up to be conned. Likewise, if a lady says in a syrupy sweet accent, "I just don't know much about anything," you may be in for a surprise. Most people don't volunteer negative information — unless they have an ulterior motive in mind.

The IRS

. . . is your partner for life. Putting aside your hard-earned dollars for Uncle Sam is your responsibility. If you receive a refund check on your income tax return, spend it wisely. Many people let the IRS withhold extra money from each paycheck just so they'll have a sizeable "bonus" check once a year. This can go into long-term or short-term savings — or you can buy yourself a special present. Whatever you decide to do, remember it's your money. Put it to good use!

Break away

. . . from it all. Everyone needs a hide-out to get away from the phone, the kids, the job or whatever. Find a quiet place to be alone and hang out a big "do not disturb" sign. You'll find the commotion of daily life much easier to face after you've had a mini-getaway.

Looks

. . . can be deceiving. A wealthy person could walk into your life dressed like a bum. Or a person wearing expensive clothes could be carrying all his wealth on his back. Judging a person's status in life by the clothes he wears is a mistake.

Friends to the end

In a perfect world, your acquaintances would turn out to be friends for life. Unfortunately, that's not the case. Interests, lifestyles and values change. If your best friend falls in love with your fiance, what should you do? Talk about the problem directly and honestly. If you can't resolve things, there may have to be a parting of the ways. It's sad, but it happens. Just remember, there's a whole world of people out there who could potentially be your friends.

Tom & Jerry

. . . can provide the perfect adult escape. After a rough day at work, it's fun to come home and watch the cartoons. Watching Rocky & Bullwinkle, Mickey Mouse and Bugs Bunny can give your mind a break, so you can unwind and forget about the day's problems. If you start giggling like a kid, you know your stress is gone!

DIETING

Eat fat, remain fat.

— ◆ —

Having one diet lapse is no reason
to go hog wild!

— ◆ —

You are what you eat.

— ◆ —

Dieting usually produces the least
positive results.

— ◆ —

Eat to live — don't live to eat.

— ◆ —

Be healthy — eat right, stay fit and
look good.

Sexual situations

Sexual harassment is one of the most talked about issues. Whether you're a man or woman, you need to be sure you conduct yourself appropriately. Sexual innuendos, unwanted advances, propositions and too much touching are no longer acceptable on the job — or anywhere else. The best solution may be to keep your mind on your business, your hands to yourself and your mouth closed!

The perfect plan

. . . may change without any advance notice. Maybe you've spent months planning your Hawaiian vacation, but the day before you leave an earthquake hits the island. Maybe you bought a new outfit for the office holiday party, only to come down with pneumonia. All your planning won't protect you from the unexpected. Circumstances change and some plans do fall through. Don't become frustrated about things that were not meant to be.

Always a bridesmaid

If you've never been a bride (or a groom), getting married isn't all that difficult. Once you've met someone special, marriage can soon become a natural outcome. In fact, many people like marriage so much they try it three or four times. The real catch isn't getting hitched — it's staying married.

Update your values

Are you holding on to beliefs and attitudes from the past that no longer apply to your current lifestyle? Outdated values can keep you from enjoying the present. It is essential to update your thinking periodically. Times change — and so should you.

Toot your own horn

If you don't tell the world about your accomplishments, nobody else will. There is no harm in promoting yourself — in letting others know about your skills, talents and abilities. Toot your own horn in a confident, professional manner, without sounding arrogant or boastful. It's the best form of advertising money can't buy.

Keeping up

. . . with the Joneses is a losing battle. Instead of being happy with what you have, you keep wanting more, more, more. Why let your competitive feelings control your life? It's not worth the financial and emotional stress. After all, no matter how high you climb or how much wealth you accumulate, someone in the world is always richer than you. If you're not enjoying life, then you've paid too high a price for your success.

Idle chatter

. . . and sensationalism sell the tabloids, but undercut your friendships. Gossip is something to avoid in social situations. You can talk about your own life, but avoid revealing personal facts about others. Your friends will consider you a trustworthy person — because it's true.

The ultimate insult?

Why is it when a romantic partner says, "Let's just be friends," most people believe they have received one of life's greatest insults? It would be far better to take it as a compliment. After all, friends are one of the riches in life. Hold them in the highest esteem.

Frequent fliers

. . . gain more than "brownie points" with the airlines. They're eligible for discounts on travel, hotel rooms and rental cars, as well as other incentive awards. If you spend a lot of time in the air, be sure you register as a frequent flier and keep track of those points. It costs you nothing to apply and the rewards can be great. Fly like an eagle — always alert to opportunities.

KNOWLEDGE

Wisdom is the accumulation of knowledge.

— ◆ —

You can be taught, but you must learn by yourself.

— ◆ —

Knowing something doesn't mean knowing what to do with it.

— ◆ —

Knowledge is power when used in the right way.

— ◆ —

Learning is a life-long process.

— ◆ —

Listen to your family, but make your own decisions.

Act naturally

Why pretend to be someone you're not? It's hard work to put on an act for others, and eventually your true self will emerge. Instead of pretending, act naturally and just be yourself. If you don't like the person you are, think about what qualities you would like to acquire. Then, do whatever it takes to become a better person.

Tough guys

. . . finish last. If you're a macho man or an independent woman who never asks for assistance, it's time to break out of your "Lone Ranger" mentality. Asking for help is not a sign of weakness, but an indication of strong self-esteem. Everyone has times of need, but only a confident person can ask for help. Pretending you're self-sufficient only keeps you distant from other people. If you need assistance, call out the cavalry!

Check it out

Don't assume that a person with a title or diploma has bona fide credentials. Unfortunately, there are fraudulent physicians, attorneys and other professionals who misrepresent themselves. If you have any doubt about the person, check it out with a state licensing board, a trade association or people who use their services. Don't be afraid to ask questions. An honest person has nothing to fear.

Possessed by possessions

Forget the famous bumper sticker from the '80s: "He who dies with the most toys wins." The object of the game of life is not to accumulate so many possessions, but to contribute something of value to the world. Remember that all possessions carry price tags, but people are priceless.

Promotions

. . . are to be savored. Somehow, the morning coffee tastes better in a new, larger office. Depositing a bigger paycheck is one sign of success. Some people feel guilty about their advancement — don't be one of them! You worked hard for the promotion, and now your responsibilities have grown. So, enjoy the perks that come with your new position. You've earned it!

A fresh appearance

Makeup is a practical and effective tool for improving your looks. For thousands of years, men and women have been applying substances to skin and hair to cover flaws and enhance outstanding features. Used properly, makeup can transform an ordinary face into a cover model. But used incorrectly, you could end up looking ridiculous. When it comes to cosmetics, less can often be more!

Dating

. . . is like building a snowman. You have to go through a lot of flakes before a magical Frosty comes to life. But the dating process doesn't have to be cold and miserable. Look at dating as a form of companion shopping, where you can sample many different potential partners. When the right person appears, the sun will shine and the flakes will melt away.

WORK

Successful people recognize the
difference between a job and
a career.

— ◆ —

Work doesn't always
bring rewards.

— ◆ —

Know all your options before
taking action.

— ◆ —

It's not how hard you work,
but what you accomplish.

— ◆ —

Resumes are for business,
not your social life.

— ◆ —

Learn the difference between
work and play.

TV violence

There's a dead body in the living room, but nobody seems to mind. A minute later it's replaced by a commercial for laundry detergent. The level of TV violence seems to keep rising, both in factual newscasts and fictional dramas. As a concerned viewer, you can protest by writing the stations and producers — or taking a hatchet to your picture tube. If people ask why you've taken such a violent step, just tell them you saw it on TV!

Congratulations

. . . are always appropriate. When someone you know is featured in a newspaper or magazine, clip out the article and send it with a congratulatory note. A news story doesn't need a big headline to be important to your friend or associate. This is an excellent way to stay in touch — everyone likes being noticed.

Never interrupt

. . . when someone else is speaking. It's rude to jump into a conversation before the speaker is finished. When you interrupt, you usually put both feet firmly in your mouth. You also encourage other people to follow your example and interrupt before you've completed your thoughts. Patience is one of the conversational virtues — whatever you have to say can wait.

Alimony

. . . is the high cost of leaving! After a marriage breaks up, the judge will determine your financial obligations to your ex-spouse. You could find yourself moving to a smaller residence or cutting back on your spending, but that's the price you pay for your freedom. Divorce doesn't come cheaply — either emotionally or financially.

Daydreaming

. . . is fine on an occasional basis. But chasing elusive fantasies can be a way of avoiding reality. If you dream of Tahiti from 9 to 5, chances are your job will suffer. If you spend your savings buying lottery tickets, odds are all you'll have is a drawer full of worthless paper. Give up your unattainable fantasies, so you can achieve your down-to-earth goals. Real life is far more fulfilling than even a vivid technicolor fantasy.

Shortcuts

. . . save time and energy. There's no reason to blaze a new trail at every opportunity. Take advantage of the guidance provided by others. In many situations, someone else has already found the solution — all you have to do is apply it to the problem. That's using your head.

Front-line tactics

On the battlefield, it's shoot or be shot. Fortunately, in peacetime, you have more options. If you feel you are facing impending danger, you can avoid confrontation by changing your course. Don't look for trouble when you can walk around it.

In love with love

Do you love the person you're with, or are you just in love with being in love? Sometimes, it's hard to tell the difference. You may enjoy being swept away by passion, only to realize you don't care a bit about your companion. If so, it's time to have a heart-to-heart talk with yourself. Pretend you're playing tennis and change the way you play the game. After all, a score of love-love in tennis equals two big zeros.

The walls have ears

Personal conversations are best done in private. You never know who is sitting at the next table or standing a few feet away. If you're in a public place and need to have a confidential talk, lower your voice and avoid using names. If someone appears to be eavesdropping, you can change the topic or make up a story that will confuse your uninvited listener. Then, continue your talk in a more private setting.

Keep your resume

. . . current. You never know when you'll be looking for a new job or when a career opportunity will present itself. Having an up-to-date resume available gives you a head start on the other applicants. The best job offers usually come along when you're not looking. Every few months add the latest information to your resume.

SINGLES

No one needs to apologize for
being single.

— ◆ —

Become a me, before a we.

— ◆ —

Single life can be the best of times
or the worst of times,
it's up to you.

— ◆ —

Companion shopping is just
one facet of single life.

— ◆ —

Know the rules of the game, but
know when to break them.

— ◆ —

Being single doesn't mean
being alone.

Make no mistakes

. . . when considering commitments. Ending a long-term relationship is a difficult, painful process. Sometimes in the heat of passion or the blindness of love, people make promises they soon regret. Going slow is the wisest policy. Make sure both your heart and your head are in agreement. Remember that making a commitment is much easier than getting out of one.

Ding-a-lings

You rush to the phone only to find no one on the other end. It's really annoying. But thanks to the phone company's new technology, you can readily identify the mystery caller or set your phone to call the number back. If you're still using your old Princess phone, consider upgrading your service to take advantage of all the new features. Put your telephone's brains to work for you.

A second wind

You come home exhausted after a hard day at work. Your kids want attention, your spouse wants dinner and all you want is a few minutes of peace. Make sure your agenda comes first. Put your feet up, relax and get your second wind. A few minutes may be all it takes before you're ready to face the household tasks at hand. Rather than snarling at your family, you'll feel like smiling!

Age is only

. . . a state of mind. When you're 20, then 30 seems really old. When someone is 40, then 65 seems a long way off. Even at age 70, the next 25 years can look pretty exciting. Your chronological age matters little compared to your mental age. If you think and feel young, you'll stay young.

Seeing the light

A seasoned traveler avoids lugging heavy suitcases through the airport. Traveling light makes much better sense. Pack only the essentials. If you forget something, you can always buy it later. A vacation or business trip is always more manageable when you "see the light."

Turncoats and traitors

Few things are more unsettling than when a "friend" becomes an "enemy." It's hard to understand when trust turns into betrayal. Most people put up their guard after this unexpected turn of events. They become overly suspicious of everyone and start imagining that more treachery is coming. But remember that one bad apple doesn't have to spoil the whole bushel.

RELATIONSHIPS

The most important part of a
relationship is to relate.

— ◆ —

Partnerships have two parts
— give and take.

— ◆ —

Relationships are difficult to make,
but easy to break.

— ◆ —

You must trust to be trusted.

— ◆ —

Good relationships are not created
overnight.

— ◆ —

Respect must be earned, it
cannot be bought.

Predicament, quandary, dilemma

These fancy words all mean the same thing. But the real problem may be refusing to admit that something is wrong. If you're having difficulty with some aspect of your life, the first step forward is realizing that you have a problem. Only then, can you begin the work of solving whatever is troubling you. Hiding your head in the sand and pretending everything is all right doesn't work for anyone.

Overlook minor irritations

Keep the minor irritations of life in perspective. Red traffic lights, busy signals on the telephone and taxis that arrive five minutes late are certainly annoying. But compared with a life-threatening illness, a burglary or a traffic accident, they're minor irritations. Ask yourself, "will this really matter in another few days?" If the answer is no, then don't get emotionally worked up about it. Save your adrenaline for the big events!

Child care

Not everyone is suited to take care of children. If you're a parent, evaluate babysitters, housekeepers and day care staff carefully before making a decision. Check references, talk to other parents and inspect the physical facilities several times. Let your child meet the babysitter or see the day care center at least once before making your choice. It's your own decision, but a child's feedback can be invaluable.

Right or wrong

Sometimes there are more than two sides to an argument. You say the sorbet tastes like lemon. Your waiter says it's grapefruit. Then you read the menu — and it's really pineapple. One of the lessons of life is that sometimes both people can be wrong.

Diamonds

. . . are a girl's best friend. What a silly notion! There's no way a chunk of colorless carbon will comfort a broken heart. It's foolish to substitute an inanimate object for the pleasures of true love. Why cherish something that can't hug you back?

Raise the issue

When it comes time to ask for a salary increase, do you get cold feet? Most people put off asking the big question because they worry that the boss might resent the request and make life difficult. Before you ask for a raise, look at your performance and how your company is doing this year. If things are going well, then pick the right time and speak up. You may be surprised at how smoothly it goes.

Forgive and forget

A good memory is a wonderful advantage in life — if used wisely. It enables you to recall important people, places and events from the past. Unfortunately, many people choose to dwell on the mistakes made by others. It's difficult to get along with someone who remembers only past hurts and errors. A great relationship develops when people learn to forgive and forget.

Aim carefully

Taking a shotgun approach to life can be frustrating. If you're trying to hit too many targets at the same time, and scattering all your shots, it's time for a different weapon. Try using a rifle and focus all your energy on one goal at a time. Once you have accomplished that objective, then move on to the next. Be a "sharpshooter" and you'll be more likely to reach your personal goals.

Speaking in tongues

In today's global economy, the more languages you speak, the better. When you meet people from different countries, you can greet them in their own language. Understanding their culture and history helps you find a common ground for friendship or a business relationship. The world is a big place. Language is the link that brings people together.

Flirting

. . . is a skill, not a genetic trait. You too, can learn how to start a friendly conversation with a stranger, make eye contact with someone interesting across a crowded room or flash a dazzling smile. Like other social skills, flirting improves with practice — and it's fun! Being able to flirt, when appropriate, improves your confidence and self-esteem. You can say a lot with a wink or a nod!

SUCCESS

Winners are doers — losers
are dreamers.

— ◆ —

Accept success, don't try
to define it.

— ◆ —

Know the difference between
temptation and opportunity.

— ◆ —

In order to succeed — act successful.

— ◆ —

Don't create a standard of
perfection that is impossible
to achieve.

— ◆ —

Success is achieved by people who
won't accept failure.

Kidding around

Deep inside, almost everybody wants to be a kid again. Childhood usually brings back memories of an uncomplicated time, when your hopes and ambitions were high. You probably felt capable of conquering the world. These childlike feelings are still there. Try getting in touch with the "kid" inside you, the child who knows how to have fun and to dream. It could be like finding a long-lost friend.

The right notes

Your mood is often influenced by music. The rhythm and melody of a song can soothe or stimulate your emotional state. If you're feeling romantic, put on the violins. If you're feeling low, try listening to a brass band or an upbeat "golden oldie." At the end of a long, tiring day, some quiet jazz or classical music might help you unwind. As your moods change through the day, let music help you.

First impressions

. . . leave lasting feelings. To make a good impression during those first 30 seconds, pay close attention to the basics — your overall appearance, handshake and conversational skills — or you'll turn people off. If you want people to get to know the inner you, first pay attention to the outer you.

The test of friendship

If you fall in love, you may lose a friend. The hardest test of friendship comes after you've told your unattached pals that you've found your future mate. They'll be happy for you — but they know things won't be the same. Rather than thinking about the "old gang" breaking up, focus on the positive. They won't be losing a friend, but gaining a new one.

Eating right

. . . is just as easy as eating wrong. It takes the same time and effort in the supermarket to pick out nutritious foods as it does to select junk food. In many cases the "convenience" items lack essential nutrients. They are also more expensive. The basic healthy foods are still your best buys.

Leopards don't change

. . . their spots. If your partner is a sports fanatic, don't expect him to miss the game. If she lives to shop, then be sure to include an outlet mall on your next trip. When it comes to people, what you see is what you get. Yes, some people do change for the better — sometimes. But don't hold your breath waiting for a zebra to lose its stripes.

But enough about me

Let's talk about you: "What do you think of me?" Some people only talk about themselves. Their conversations always begin with I, and leave no room for another person. If everyone scatters when you open your mouth, it's time to drop that self-centered approach. Start showing an interest in other people. Ask questions about their lives. Everyone likes to be acknowledged — and you will soon be welcomed into conversations. If you hope to win friends and influence people, this is the way to go.

LAW

Prisons are filled with perfect alibis.

— ◆ —

If you do the crime — pay the time.

— ◆ —

Never sign a legal document
without a magnifying glass.

— ◆ —

Laws are designed to protect
the innocent.

— ◆ —

Every fact has three interpretations
— yours, mine and the truth.

— ◆ —

There's always a price to pay when
there's foul play.

Like wine

. . . relationships either get better with age or go sour. To avoid having your relationship spoil, take time to think about your behavior and make any needed adjustments. A good starting place is to show your partner more love and appreciation. In a fast-paced world, it's easy to take someone for granted. Instead, keep your partner right at the top of your list. Think about how you would like to be treated — and do the same.

Invest in yourself

. . . and collect the dividends. Start setting time aside for personal improvement. Enroll in an educational class, go to the health club or learn a new professional skill. Make yourself a priority. Like a good stock, you'll soon start rising in value!

Why replay the past?

Maybe your life would have changed if you'd caught that touchdown pass in high school. But the fact is you dropped the ball. All the wishing in the world can't change the past. So, why replay it in your mind. It's much healthier to enjoy today and set goals for tomorrow.

Insurance

. . . is one of the few purchases you hope never to use. No one wants to be hospitalized or smash a car to see how well they're protected. But it's important to select the right types of coverage from the many options available. Too much or too little insurance can be costly. Be a smart shopper and review your coverage on a regular basis. Insurance isn't a fun subject, but it's fun-damental to your financial plans.

Knock, knock

Opportunity can arrive unannounced on your doorstep at any time. Will you open the door when it arrives? Many people expect a social or business opportunity to announce itself and show up precisely on time. In fact, nearly all opportunities are unexpected. Be flexible enough to recognize them and seize the moment.

Take heed

. . . when a friend is in need. Friendship is tested in hard times. When you're on a winning streak, everyone wants to be your buddy. But when the tide turns, your acquaintances will disappear while your true friends remain. And it's when times are tough that you appreciate them the most.

Perspiration

Success in life is due far more to perspiration than inspiration. It's relatively simple to start a project, but courage, endurance and persistence are needed to see it through to completion. Once you have accomplished your task, give yourself a pat on the back. Your next endeavor is more likely to succeed because you have a track record of persistence.

Sticky notes

. . . can keep you from getting stuck at home, as well as in the office. Post your notes for the family on the refrigerator. If you're mailing a package, add a note instead of a long letter. If you visit a friend and no one's there, leave a note on the door. Always "stick" a note or two in your billfold, and never leave home without them!

It is impossible

. . . to be in two places at the same time. That's why you must develop a personal organizational system. Never rely on your memory to tell you where you need to be or when you are expected. Write your schedule down and keep an up-to-date appointment book. That way you'll always arrive on schedule at the correct location.

Throw a party

. . . for no reason at all. Don't wait for a special occasion — just invite your friends over for a get-together. You could plan a theme party and have everyone dress in costume. Or commemorate another country's national holiday, and serve Swedish meatballs, Japanese tempura or Irish stew. Plan an event that's fun to give and puts no strain on your budget. A party is really something to celebrate!

Behavior

To understand a person's behavior,
look for the cause.

— ◆ —

One on one is the best way to
settle differences.

— ◆ —

Set an example and others
will follow.

— ◆ —

A threat is only as good as the
person who makes it.

— ◆ —

Know when to complain and
when to praise.

— ◆ —

Good behavior has its rewards.

Regrets

. . . are a natural part of life. At times, everyone thinks about what could have or should have happened. But don't dwell on the past that you cannot change. It's much healthier to think about ways to improve your present life. Time marches forward, and you need to stay in step.

Moonlighting

. . . can be more than just an excellent way to fatten your bank account. It can expand your social and professional horizons as well. Taking on part-time work in a new field can point you in a different career direction. At the very least, it can be a refreshing change in your daily routine.

Turning green

Envy can creep up on you and attack without warning. Your best friend buys a new car and rather than being happy about it, you wish someone would steal it. Another friend gets engaged and you wish it were you instead. When jealousy and envy take control of your better judgment, you may do things you'll regret. Don't give in to the green-eyed monster.

Leave a message

Answering machines are here to stay. When leaving your name, number and message be sure to speak slowly and clearly. Keep your message short and to the point. Don't say anything you might regret later on. After all, you never know who else might be listening.

Tricked by trappings

Are you attracted to luxury cars, designer clothes and fast boats? Be careful, or you'll be tricked by the trappings in life. People afflicted with this disease accept or reject others solely on the basis of wealth (or at least the appearance of wealth). The only cure is to give up the glitter and glamour for the true wealth of friendship!

SELF

Take responsibility for
your actions.

— ◆ —

Self-improvement is an
ongoing goal.

— ◆ —

Sing your own praises, but be
prepared to defend them.

— ◆ —

A clear conscience has no
trouble sleeping.

— ◆ —

Only a fool allows fantasy to
replace reality.

— ◆ —

Self-recommendation is no
recommendation.

A good excuse

. . . is one that's believable. If you turn down an invitation saying you're going to the baseball game, be certain that the team is playing at home. A pair of tickets provides a reasonable excuse — but if you tell the hostess you'll be out of town and she sees you at the grocery store, your credibility will be shot. If you need to say no, make sure your answer is plausible.

Below the belt

Faced with a challenge, some people resort to below-the-belt tactics, like lying and ridiculing. There is never any reason to resort to dishonest or immature behavior to get what you want. If you are tempted to behave like a child, stop yourself. Back off until you are in control of your feelings. Otherwise, you'll regret tomorrow what you did today.

Increase business

. . . by acting professionally and developing a likeable personality. While it's important to have a skill or expertise in what you do, it's just as important for others to feel comfortable around you. When you can carry on a conversation and put others at ease, you're well on the way to success. It's easier to catch flies with honey than vinegar.

Fact or fiction

Separating fact from fiction is a difficult task in the land of TV "docudramas" and computerized "editing" of photographs. You just can't believe everything you see or hear. Some people are skilled at telling untruths or half-truths for their own purposes. Consider the source of the information and the reasons for sending it — are they selling something? Do the best you can to read between the lines.

The middle ages

. . . should be a period of renaissance. Here's an opportunity to reflect on what you've accomplished so far, set new goals for the future and create a more satisfying lifestyle. You have both the energy and the maturity to enjoy this phase on your life's journey. Best of all, the "golden years" are yet to come.

Passion

Life without passion is like a day without sunshine — gray, dreary and utterly boring. Think about what really turns you on — another person, a challenging task, an exciting vacation or helping others. Then, follow your passion! Let it be your guide as you wander through the valleys of life. Passion will give you the courage to climb the highest mountains and swim the deepest seas. Treasure that feeling!

Moving forward

If a job change requires you to relocate, the moving van may arrive too soon. It's hard to say goodbye to your old friends and leave your home. But there's also a bright side. It's always an adventure to move to a new community and make a fresh start. If moving is a must, pack your furniture, but leave your troubles behind!

To make a point

There must be a point. It's difficult to have a conversation with someone who never stays on track. If all your conversations keep running off the rails, try to focus on one subject at a time. Think about what you want to say, then say it. The direct approach is better than beating around the bush.

Bite your tongue

. . . and count to 10 before blasting away. If you have a hair-trigger temperament, keep the safety catch on. Nobody likes to be the target of a fault-finding barrage. Negative comments and disparaging remarks are destructive. What's on your mind doesn't necessarily need to be on your tongue!

MARRIAGE

A marriage made in heaven is not
made in haste.

— ◆ —

The perfect mate is not always the
perfect person.

— ◆ —

It takes two to make a marriage,
but only one to break it.

— ◆ —

Marriage is a merger — not
an acquisition.

— ◆ —

A wedding is not the
ultimate answer.

— ◆ —

New ideas can improve an
old marriage.

Duplicates

When you entrust the postal service or package company with your important documents, be sure to make a copy for yourself. Keep the duplicate in a safe, easily accessible location. You never know when you'll need the extra. A copy that takes only seconds to make could save you hours of grief.

Two halves

. . . don't make a whole. It's foolish to spend your life searching for someone who will make you feel complete. Only you can make yourself whole — no one else has that power. So, concentrate on becoming a better person who is happy being single. Then, when you finally connect with someone special, a different formula will apply — two wholes that each make half of a marriage.

Change your habits

Everyone needs a change of pace now and then. It's easy to fall into a rut. If you find your life is getting predictable, break out of your routine and try something new. You'll find yourself getting excited, enthusiastic and energized again!

If it's worth having

. . . it's worth the wait. Many people want "instant" gratification, and can't bear the thought of having to wait for something. But like a child who learns to wait 12 months for the next birthday, you too can learn a little patience. All good things come to those who wait.

The space race

When you're in a torrid romance, the last thing you want is to be alone. You think about your partner constantly, spend every possible minute together and call at all hours of the day and night. If your significant other requests some time alone, you take it as complete rejection. To avoid burning out a red-hot passion, respect your partner's right to privacy. Too much "crowding" in a relationship is likely to result in a race for some personal space.

Teasing or taunting?

Nearly everyone can handle teasing, provided it's done in good spirit. Sometimes, though, teasing can cross the line into taunting. Then, it's no fun for anyone. Don't let humor become an assault weapon. Would you find the joke just as funny if you were the target? If not, try being a mime instead of a clown.

Getting a pink slip

. . . can be a shattering experience. But it can also open the door to new opportunities. A layoff can give you time to examine your goals, discover what you really want from a career and find a new job that makes you happier than the last one. A pink slip can also be a launching pad for your own business, as it was for many successful entrepreneurs. Take advantage of whatever comes your way!

Look before you leap

Don't make important decisions in a split second. Take enough time to make up your mind. Someone in your life may be pushing for a quick decision, but if you're not ready, resist that pressure. If they really care about you, they will understand and respect your needs. Too many adults spend years regretting instant decisions.

CONVERSATION

Anyone can start a conversation,
but not everyone can
end it gracefully.

— ◆ —

Gossip was invented by people who
have nothing to say.

— ◆ —

Wait to be asked before
you answer.

— ◆ —

The best results are produced
by listening.

— ◆ —

The tone of your voice can say
more than words.

— ◆ —

Communication is the purpose
for conversation.

The state of your estate

. . . should be one of your financial concerns. Take time to prepare a will, determine how your possessions should be divided and write out your final wishes. A sound estate plan can reduce taxes and help your loved ones know what you really wanted. And this is the last chance you'll have to do things your way!

Man's best friend

. . . isn't always a dog. If you are an animal lover, it's hard to accept that others don't share your passion. Many people will go to great lengths to avoid a close encounter of the doggie kind. Respect their wishes and don't force them to become friends with Fido.

Time out

Every so often, you need to call time out. Take a look at yourself and evaluate how you are doing. Are you happy? What changes do you want to make? Where do you hope to be next year? Only by asking yourself questions will you discover the answers.

Happily ever after

Only in fairy tales do Cinderella and Prince Charming live happily ever after. In real life, they would probably argue about staying out too late at the ball, spending too much on gowns and slippers, and who cleans up after the clock strikes midnight. Fairy tales and modern romance novels make good reading, but don't ever confuse a story with reality. You can live happily ever after, as long as you recognize that life is filled with ups and downs — and accept the rough spots with the smooth.

Make requests

. . . not demands. Would you rather
be asked — or told — to do something? Making demands is one of the
best ways to turn other people off.
It's best to make clear, concise
requests. The more specific, the
better. Your request will be heard,
even if it isn't granted. Demands
usually fall on deaf ears.

RSVP

When an invitation arrives, respond promptly. As soon as you know whether you will be attending or not, send the answer back with your reply card. It is aggravating to your hosts if you ignore the invitation or wait until the last minute to provide them with a simple "oui" or "non."

Work and play

After a grinding day at the office, you need time to unwind. The best way to combat job burnout is to make time for personal interests and recreational activities. Don't feel guilty about relaxing. You'll work more productively the next day by taking time to play today.

Defensive driving

. . . is one of the fundamental rules behind the wheel. You never know who's driving that car next to yours — it could easily be someone intoxicated, impaired or unskilled. Stay alert at all times while driving and expect the unexpected. Give yourself room to maneuver and always watch out for the other guy!

Shop till you drop

If you're one of those people who live to shop, try to control your impulses. Chances are your partner won't spend hours holding your bags while you try on clothes. Shop by yourself or with someone who shares your obsession. That way you can prevent your relationship from going "on sale."

PARENTING AND CHILDREN

To be a good parent doesn't always mean saying "yes".

— ◆ —

Give children choices that you can live with.

— ◆ —

Perfect parents are not born, they evolve.

— ◆ —

Teach your children too well and you may end up eating your words.

— ◆ —

Don't forget — parents are people.

— ◆ —

Other people's children are a joy to behold.

Joys of cooking

There's an antidote for fast-fooditis. It's called staying at home and cooking your own dinner. Besides offering a chance to cut down on the high cost of restaurants, cooking at home allows you to eat a healthier, better balanced diet. You can have fun by trying new recipes and developing your own dishes. And there's something about the smell of bread baking in the oven that turns any house into a home. Bon appetit!

Three strikes

. . . and you're out. This rule from the world of baseball should also apply to your life. If you make a mistake the first time, try again. Everyone deserves a second chance. But make sure you succeed — if you strike out a third time, it's all over.

Value your valuables

No one is safe from the break-in artist. A skilled burglar can deal with even the most sophisticated locks and alarm systems. That's why having a safety deposit box at a bank is a smart move. Keep your valuables and important papers away from sticky fingers.

Ignorance is bliss

You are mesmerized by someone who has a flaw. But rather than accept that imperfection, you try to change it. It nags at you until it begins to dominate your entire relationship. At that point you have a choice — either end the relationship or forget about the flaw. What you can't change, you can at least learn to ignore.

Count your blessings

No one else will! One excellent way to improve your disposition is to take a periodic inventory of all the good things life has to offer — past, present and future. You may be surprised to discover how many things are on your list. There's no need to wait for that special day in November to give thanks and count your blessings.

Nothing like a name

You appreciate it when someone remembers your name. So does everyone else. When you meet a person, be sure to repeat the name correctly. If you have trouble remembering names verbally, ask for a business card or write the name down later with some identifying information. The name of the game is to remember names!

Live in harmony

It's far better to live in peace with your neighbors than to exist in a constant state of turmoil. Trouble usually starts with a small incident that gets blown out of proportion. Before it reaches the stage of threats and possible violence, talk to each other. Discuss the differences and see if they can be resolved. Fighting with the folks next door is like a marriage gone bad — except you can't divorce your neighbors.

Style or fashion?

Fashionable new clothes line the racks of department stores and boutiques. But choosing styles that flatter can be tricky. An outfit which looks great on the hanger may not be the right one for you. By cultivating your own sense of style, you can identify what makes you look best. Fashion fads come and go, but your personal style can last a lifetime.

Friendship

. . . is like a flower. You can plant a seed, but whether it grows or not depends on the attitudes and actions taken by two people. But if you provide the right time, effort and attention, there is a good chance the friendship will mature and blossom. A good friendship is like a flower — a thing of beauty.

Special moments

. . . should be shared with your significant other — not with the world. There's little to be gained by telling your inner circle about everything that happens. Instead, respect your partner's privacy and keep those special moments confidential. Develop your own private history of shared memories and experiences. Don't short-change yourself by turning your life into an open book.

DIVORCE

Marriage is a mystery, but divorce
is an open book.

— ◆ —

You don't know what you'll miss
until it disappears.

— ◆ —

Before you separate on impulse,
consider the alternatives.

— ◆ —

You can divorce your mate, but not
your children.

— ◆ —

End a relationship with the same
style in which it began.

— ◆ —

Divorce can be a costly mistake.

Earth Days

Ecology is more than a trendy buzzword. It's a way for all of us to live in harmony with the Earth's plants and animals. You have the opportunity each day to do something to protect the environment. Start a garden. Ride a bicycle. Install a solar-energy system. Make it a point to celebrate Earth Day every day of the year.

Praise in public

But criticize in private. The best time to point out someone's faults or to air your frustrations is behind closed doors. Picking a public forum to chastise someone leads only to embarrassment and humiliation — and makes it far more difficult for the other person to listen and accept your point of view. If you can't say something nice in public, then zip your lips.

Gamble only

. . . what you can afford to lose. Betting at the track, feeding a slot machine or playing poker can be an exciting experience. But the odds are against you becoming a winner. Don't get carried away by a lucky streak and bet more than you can afford. The "luckiest" gamblers are those who know when to quit.

A balanced decision

. . . requires objectivity. When you are emotionally involved with someone or something, it's difficult to maintain an objective viewpoint. That's why a surgeon won't operate on a family member and an attorney won't represent himself. Don't let your feelings and personal biases influence your major decisions.

Muggers and thieves

. . . are in every city. Take plenty of precautions to foil muggers, pickpockets and scoundrels. Carry only the credit cards you plan to use that day. Put your cash, driver's license and plastic in separate places. That way if someone grabs your wallet, the damage will be minimized. Just remember that anything the robbers take can be replaced — except your life.

Reality checks

Have you ever gotten a great idea at 3 a.m. that turned out to be useless the next day? Most people have sudden brainstorms, ideas or thoughts that need a reality check. Before you go off the deep end, talk to an expert for a second opinion. If it's a great idea, you can still go ahead. If not, you haven't lost any time or energy pursuing an impractical endeavor.

Close to culture

Are you intimidated by cultural snobs — the experts who seem to know everything about the fine arts? If so, you could be overlooking an exciting adventure right in your own community. There's nothing like the joy of discovering a whole new realm you overlooked. Get closer to culture, and broaden your horizons.

PAST

History has a habit of
repeating itself.

— ◆ —

Don't dwell on the past, it's a
closed book.

— ◆ —

Sometimes memories are better
than the real thing.

— ◆ —

Yesterday went astray, but
tomorrow holds promise
for the future.

— ◆ —

It's not necessary to advertise
your past.

— ◆ —

The future lives on, long after the
memories are gone.

Single(*)

Not every single you meet is unattached. Many unmarried people are involved in committed relationships or live together like husband and wife without the marriage license. When someone tells you "I'm single," determine if there's an asterisk attached. Otherwise, your assumptions could get you into an embarrassing situation.

Mapmaker, mapmaker

. . . make me a map! When you give complicated directions by telephone, you're likely to confuse the other person. Instead, why not create a simple map and fax it. This forces you to think about the best route to take and avoids time-consuming explanations. Best of all, it greatly increases the odds that the other person will arrive on time.

Turn off the TV

Many shy people use the television to escape from the real world. Rather than risk meeting new people, they settle into a familiar nightly routine. There is only one solution for "couch potato-itis." Turn off the TV! Then, pick up your phone to call a friend or get in your car and go somewhere. You'll discover a world far more exciting than the latest sitcom.

Rags to riches

It wasn't easy growing up on the wrong side of the tracks. Just getting enough food and clothing was a challenge. Today, things are different. Your abilities have carried you to the top. Be thankful for everything you have gained. But don't lose the most important thing — the common touch.

Your body

. . . needs to last a lifetime. Yet many people seem set on a self-destructive course, smoking, drinking or eating to excess. Why shorten your life? It's much better to take good care of your body. Your cells will thank you for it!

A taxing situation

When April 15th rolls around, you face a choice. Either prepare an honest income tax return or try to stretch the truth. In this high-tech era, it's easy for the Internal Revenue to uncover any discrepancies, so why be tempted to cheat? If you are honest in filling out your return, you have nothing to fear from an audit. If you cheat, your misdeeds will hang over your head for years.

Public speaking

... is one of the most widespread fears in the world. Even professional speakers get nervous when faced with a live audience. Nevertheless, a successful public appearance can do wonders for your self-image. The secret is rehearsal. Get plenty of practice before you get up on stage. You know your topic better than anyone in the audience. Make eye contact, remember your note cards and keep smiling. Your audience will think you've been a public speaker all your life!

Alone again

You can't always be surrounded by others. Yet, some people refuse to go to the movies alone or eat at a restaurant without a companion. If you dislike soloing in public, you're missing an opportunity to enjoy time on your own. When you're alone you can do just what you want. That can be a liberating feeling!

In-laws are people

. . . who deserve your respect. Make them feel welcome in your house at all times. After all, they brought your spouse into the world. Now, they're part of your family, too. Treat them with kindness, and you'll find the bonds of these new relationships growing stronger. Turn away "outlaws" — but never in-laws.

Out and about

Do you want to meet a potential friend or lover? Does your business need new customers? Unless you get out and about, you'll never meet new people. If you want to become the invisible man or woman on the social circuit, just stay home every night. Venture forth and who knows what good things will happen.

TIME

So little time, so many choices.

— ◆ —

Every day is a good day — until
you spoil it.

Use time wisely, don't just waste it.

— ◆ —

Invest in yourself and reap
the rewards.

— ◆ —

If you want to get things done,
don't procrastinate.

— ◆ —

Value another person's time as you
would your own.

Give, give, give

The best way to keep a client or strengthen a business relationship is to give all you've got. All the bill-boards in the world won't replace word-of-mouth advertising. Your customers will tell their friends about your products or services — if they're satisfied. Make them happy and your business will prosper.

Return phone calls

. . . within 24 hours. Every caller deserves a prompt response — you never know what good things could result from the conversation. If you are unable to make a quick return call, set up a support system — perhaps a colleague, family member or friend could return the calls for you. No matter where you are in the world, you're just a phone call away from your answering machine.

Fantasy or reality?

Some people read too many romance novels. They imagine themselves with an ideal partner on an enchanted island or in a medieval castle — then wonder why real life is boring. While everyone needs a touch of romance from time to time, keep your feet on solid ground. Life itself can be far more entertaining than fiction, if you let it become a "novel" experience!

Holidays

. . . aren't fun for everyone. You may love the period from Christmas to New Year's, but it's a time of extra stress for some people. They may be alone, and feel particularly lonely when everyone around them seems to be celebrating. If you know someone is suffering from the holiday blues, 'tis the season to cheer them up!

Keep the safety on

Do you carry a weapon to protect yourself? If so, be sure you know how to use it. Thousands of people are killed or injured each year in gun accidents. Make sure all weapons are stored out of reach of small children and keep ammunition in a separate location for safety. Don't let someone in your family become a statistic.

Personal ads

Can be risky business. Those well-crafted lines can be deceptive. Every writer is trying to make a "sale," so only the good points make it into print. Those extra-embellished ads could only have been written by a mother! If you decide to answer a personal, be cautious. What you read isn't always what you get!

Doctors say

. . . an annual physical exam is essential. Even if you're feeling fine, that checkup could reveal a problem at an early stage, while it's still very treatable. Medical science has come a long way, but you still need to do your part. Make an investment in your own health — your body will say thanks!

Hands tell all

Not everyone is anxious to share their age. Surgery, makeup and lies can conceal a person's birth date very effectively. So, when you are searching for an approximate age, look at a person's hands. Not surprisingly, there are many youthful faces with aged fingers and palms.

Compliments or complaints?

Would you rather work for a boss who gives you compliments or one who complains constantly? How about the people who work for you — do you distribute compliments freely? Accentuating the positive is a great way to build morale. Everyone likes to hear that a job is well done, and it makes an occasional criticism much easier to bear. A compliment from the boss can really make a difference in the workplace.

Advise and consent

When you were a teenager, your parents were constantly giving advice. Chances are you got into more trouble when you ignored them than when you followed their suggestions. As an adult, you can make all your own decisions, but sometimes it helps when a peer can advise and consent to your wishes. Maybe it's buying a new car or weighing a job offer from out of town. Asking for advice may keep you from making a foolish mistake.

EXPERIENCE

Our greatest achievements are often
our greatest embarrassments.

— ◆ —

Experience is the best teacher of all,
but it sends a terrific bill.

— ◆ —

If you have learned a lesson,
consider the knowledge valuable.

— ◆ —

Experience doesn't always get the
job done.

— ◆ —

It is just as important to know what
you cannot do as what you can.

— ◆ —

Experience is the accumulation
of mistakes.

Pack rats

. . . can't bear to throw anything away. Unfortunately, their closets are so full, they can never find what they want. If you suffer from this syndrome, recovery is only a few garbage bags away! Clean out the hope chest, the basement and the attic. Hold a yard sale or make a charitable donation. Get rid of your clutter and your home will seem bigger!

Cash is king

. . . at home or abroad. Flea market and sidewalk vendors usually don't accept plastic. Other merchants will give you a discount for paying with cash. Always carry enough cash to avoid embarrassing situations — such as having to tip a valet or a bellhop. Money talks when credit cards walk.

Speak now

. . . or forever hold your peace. That familiar line from a wedding ceremony contains a grain of truth. Ask all your questions first. Clear up any misunderstandings before you shake hands or sign on the dotted line. It's much harder to back out after you've made a commitment.

Creativity

. . . begins with an idea. Think about all the conveniences of modern life that surround you. Each began as a thought in someone's mind. As you go through your daily routine, pay attention to the ideas in your head. Inside everyone is a creative genius. Set your imagination free and see what happens!

Don't say yes

. . . when you mean no. Everyone has made this mistake, out of misguided politeness or concern for another's feelings. But if saying "yes" has become a habit, it's time to start saying "no." You may be overly sensitive to others or insensitive to yourself. It's far better to feel good about a "no" than to feel miserable about a "yes."

Reach out

. . . and touch the one you love. A hug, back rub or snuggling are basic ways to communicate. Think about how parents "talk" to a newborn infant. They cuddle and touch and rock a baby to sleep. The sense of touch is a powerful one. When you start communicating with your hands and fingers, the message will be received loud and clear!

Giving and getting

For every action in life there is a reaction — but it may not always be what you expect. If you give in order to get something back, you will often be disappointed. Many people will refuse your "gifts" or take them without reciprocating. Think about why you "give to get" and rearrange your priorities. The best gifts in life are those given with no strings attached.

Date your mate

What made you think that dating was just for singles? Married couples can enjoy planning special dates with each other. Take turns in coming up with creative and unusual activities. Attend a travel auction or rent roller skates. Take a ride on a helicopter or go canoeing. You'll probably have more fun than when you were single. And you can take your date home, and know you'll still be respected in the morning.

SOCIETY

If you're going to run around in circles, be sure they are the right circles.

— ◆ —

Add a touch of class to be at the head of the class.

— ◆ —

To belong doesn't automatically mean to be accepted.

— ◆ —

Where you go isn't as important as who you go with.

— ◆ —

Be a volunteer — but know what you're volunteering for.

— ◆ —

To fit in society — you must want to.

What goes up

. . . must come down. At times in your life, things will go better than expected. Other times, it seems like everything is crashing down around you. If you're in a rough spot, remember that it won't last forever. Life is constantly full of changes. You'll be happiest if you can minimize the low periods and stretch out the "highs" to last as long as possible.

Using your head

. . . your body or your hands can help get your point across to others. Gestures are a universal form of communication, but they differ from culture to culture. When you travel, be sure to learn the appropriate body language so you don't offend someone by a wave of your hand or a "thumbs up" signal. Only a smile means the same thing everywhere on the globe!

Crystal balls

Everyone wonders what will happen in the future. Unfortunately, a crystal ball won't help. The best predictions are made logically, based on past events and current data. They may not be as exciting as a "magical" experience, but the level of accuracy will be much higher. But instead of worrying so much about the future, try to improve your life today!

Think of television

. . . as a 24-hour houseguest — someone who's always available for entertainment, education or distraction. But if you give all your attention to this charming visitor, your family members will start to resent you. It's frustrating to be around a person whose life revolves around the remote control. Too much tuning-in is a turn-off to others.

Bits and bytes

Keep in step with technology, particularly the world of computers. Every major company depends on these hard-working machines to process information about customers, products and employees. Learning about computer capabilities and functions will increase your productivity and quality of work. Just watch out for those hard drives — sometimes they "byte!"

Choose gifts

. . . using your imagination and creativity. When selecting a present, take into consideration the lifestyle and needs of the recipient. Think about any special interests or hobbies. Then, use your imagination to find something memorable. Take time to wrap the present nicely and select the right card. Your thoughtfulness will make a lasting impression.

Equitable distribution

. . . is a term used in divorce that translates into "who gets what." After splitting up the assets, you might feel a sense of loss. But remember that no judge can take away your sense of self-worth. Negotiate the best settlement, and walk away with your head held high. You still own your most important asset — yourself.

Plastic surgery

. . . is the newest status symbol. Why keep your original nose, chin or face, when a new one can be designed just for you. Plastic surgery is a good option for those who have a need to change their appearance. But make the decision based on what you want, not because it's the latest rage.

That special someone

There is someone for everyone. If the search seems impossible, you need to persevere. Remember, the world is full of people trying to meet each other. Once you connect, it's like matching up two interlocking pieces of a jigsaw puzzle. When it's the right fit, you'll know it.

A word of caution

. . . can sometimes be taken to extremes. When you were a child, your parents said, "Don't ever talk to strangers." But as an adult it's time to reprogram your thinking. If you use good judgment, it's perfectly acceptable to start a conversation with a stranger in a suitable and safe setting. Take advantage of opportunities to approach other people and you may find that today's stranger may be tomorrow's friend or business partner.

ARGUMENTS

Know the facts before you
take a stand.

— ◆ —

In an argument — stick to the issue.

— ◆ —

Never counterattack criticism
with denial.

— ◆ —

Arguments are never won
by shouting.

— ◆ —

Negotiation is the fine art
of arguing.

— ◆ —

If you must fight — fight fair.

Network for success

Advancing in life depends more on who you know than what you know. A network of business and social contacts is a valuable resource. Always carry a stack of business cards with your name and phone number. They can be your "entree" to new opportunities. Give your cards away freely — you never know who will call back.

A great idea

The more specific the compliment, the better. Would you rather be told, "Your hair looks great" or "Your new layered hairstyle really suits the shape of your face?" It's clear that the second compliment was based on close observation, not an offhand remark. Remember that principle when talking to others.

Mr. Clean

From shining floors to spotless ceilings, your home should have Mr. Clean's stamp of approval. It's not enough to pick things up just before company arrives. A tidy, well-organized home is a more pleasant place to live — and you never have to worry about misplacing something important. Best of all, you can be proud of your home if an unexpected visitor shows up.

Seeing red

. . . is fine if you're looking at a fire engine. But it's extremely dangerous if you've just lost your temper and are out of control. Before you do something you'll regret, take a deep breath, walk away or count to three. Learning to control your anger helps you stay in charge of your actions, and will probably improve your disposition. Once you stop "seeing red," you'll no longer feel blue.

Playing with cards

Credit cards make it easy to buy now and pay later. But you're better off buying a boomerang than running up a large debt — that way you won't be surprised when things come back to hit you in the head. There's no point in turning half your paycheck over to MasterCard or Visa. Credit cards can be helpful, as long as you use them responsibly.

Fat or thin?

Inside every fat person is a thin person trying to escape. But when your eating habits are out of control, those pounds just won't go away. Eating properly and exercising regularly can help you feel better and lose weight. If you have trouble getting started, seek professional advice. Dieting is not the secret — it's learning how to change the way you eat and live.

Lift your spirits

No one needs illegal drugs to lift their spirits. When you're feeling down, take a few moments to appreciate yourself. Make a list of your talents, skills and good qualities. Remember your accomplishments, both personal and professional. Remind yourself that you have many things to offer other people. The best way to elevate your mood is to love yourself.

Breaking up

. . . is one of the hardest things to do. It's never easy to end a marriage, friendship or business relationship. When you know it's over, a wide range of emotions come into play: anger, loss, disappointment and perhaps some relief. But in the heat of the moment, resist the temptation to say hurtful things. Tearing another person down won't help to build you up.

Pencil or pen

When you're making notes in your appointment book or calendar, there's no substitute for an old-fashioned pencil. When your schedule changes, just erase what you've written. Save your pen for events that cannot possibly change, like a holiday or birthday. For the most important meetings or activities, use a highlighter as well — in this case, bright yellow means "go, go, go!"

MONEY

A bargain could be the mistake of a lifetime.

— ◆ —

Money is the bait many use when fishing for a mate.

— ◆ —

The cheaper your wants, the richer you'll be.

— ◆ —

To know the value of money, try borrowing it.

— ◆ —

Just because it's affordable doesn't mean you can afford it.

— ◆ —

If you bank on an inheritance, you may be disappointed.

Holding patterns

Stop putting your life on hold. Many people delay doing things they enjoy until a better job comes along, the kids are grown, retirement occurs — or some other excuse. Unfortunately, illness, accidents or death can disrupt those plans. Break out of that holding pattern. Your birth certificate is your passport to life!

Change

. . . is the only constant in life. Nothing ever stays the same for very long. Just because you've always done something a certain way doesn't mean it's right. Open your mind to alternatives. The only way to make progress is to embrace change. If you're standing still, you can't ever move forward!

Talking vs. doing

How much of the day do you spend thinking about what needs to be done and talking about it before actually taking action? It's pointless to waste hour after hour discussing and complaining. Instead, why not do the job enthusiastically right away, then move on to the next task. After all, the shortest distance between two points is a straight line.

Know it all

A degree from Harvard is impressive, but it doesn't make you a "know-it-all" when it comes to personal relationships. An IQ test measures intellectual abilities, but nobody has devised an "EQ test" to measure emotional abilities. Your EQ is what counts when it comes to relationships, so stay in touch with your feelings, and know when to act on them.

When disaster strikes

. . . it's too late to prepare. Earthquakes, hurricanes, blizzards and floods threaten different parts of the world. Develop your own personal disaster plan well in advance of any potential problems. Consider storing extra food and water, stocking up on batteries and flashlights, and determining where you would stay if your home were destroyed. It is always better to be prepared than to find yourself in a dangerous situation.

Too accessible

If there are times you don't want to be reached, be careful in giving out your beeper or cellular phone number. Clients, acquaintances and friends can usually live without 24-hour access to you. Let your answering machine or the fax be an alternative method of contact. Everyone needs private time — protect yours.

To fail

. . . is human. To learn from the experience is divine. When something you planned goes wrong, try to determine what happened. Maybe your plan was faulty. Maybe you made a mistake. Maybe outside conditions led to the failure. In any case, you have an excellent opportunity to study the situation, and correct any errors. For many people, a resounding failure was the first step toward ultimate success.

ATTITUDES

Respect differing viewpoints even if
you disagree.

— ◆ —

Alter your perspective and
change your life.

— ◆ —

Personal growth happens when
your outlook changes.

— ◆ —

Your mood is a reflection
of your attitude.

— ◆ —

Think positive and negative
thoughts will disappear.

— ◆ —

If you have an attitude, make it
a good one.

Fit, fitter, fittest

If you're starting an exercise program, consider hiring a personal trainer. Following the advice of an expert is one way to get started on the right foot. Your goal may be to improve your endurance, to strengthen specific muscle groups or to lose weight. In each case, a personal trainer can help you achieve the results you want.

Money, money, money

Are you in charge of your wallet —
or is your wallet in charge of you? If
you find yourself making day-to-day
decisions based primarily on money,
then you've lost sight of the big
picture. Everyone has financial
concerns, but use your common
"sense" when thinking about dollars.
Money makes a great servant, but a
poor master.

Spread too thin?

When the boss asks you for a little extra help, you'll probably say "sure." When a friend asks for a ride, it's easy to say "yes." When you hear the question, "Any volunteers?" your hand may automatically go up. But if you always say "yes," you're probably spreading yourself too thin. Unfortunately, the more you try to do, the less you accomplish. Unless you're a chipmunk, don't try to bite off more than you can chew.

Clipping coupons

. . . makes cents for some people. Depending on your lifestyle, clipping out those little paper rectangles can save money, or be a complete waste of time. If you truly need the advertised products — and no lower-priced alternatives will do — then start a coupon file and watch your savings pile up. Otherwise, this is one habit you can safely cut out!

Jelly bean logic

Is there a correct way to eat jelly beans? Some people are particular, choosing only the reds, whites or blues. They savor each jelly bean one at a time. Others just grab a big handful and quickly down them all. If life were compared to a bowl of jelly beans, you would see just as many different approaches to living. We're all individuals with a unique style.

I'm sorry

These two words are easy to say, but difficult to show. After you have insulted someone, it's easy to offer an apology. All it takes is two little words. However, they won't erase the harm you've already done. If you're sincere about wanting to make things better, "showing" is better than "telling." Find a way to convince the other person that you want to patch things up. Let your actions speak louder than your words.

Try your hardest

. . . but recognize your own limitations. The old adage "practice makes perfect" is one of those half-truths of life. In many cases endurance and dedication will pay off. But other times, no matter how much you try, you'll simply be knocking your head against the wall. Be realistic about your abilities and potential.

HAPPINESS

Happiness is a healthy
state of mind.

— ◆ —

Travel with a light heart and
joyful expectations.

— ◆ —

Why pursue happiness when you
can create it?

— ◆ —

It's a mistake to depend on others
to make you happy.

— ◆ —

The true secret of harmony is
rejoicing for someone else.

— ◆ —

Happy faces get you into all
the right places.

Consider everything

Think about all the possibilities whenever you come up with a new idea. Determining if the idea is a winner often depends on mixing your enthusiasm with a strong dose of objective thinking. Even if your idea is 99 and 44/100 percent right, look at all the angles. An ounce more of planning can prevent an unexpected surprise.

Winning a battle

What good does it do to win a battle and lose the war? Sometimes, a heated discussion turns into an argument, which then becomes a war. When fatigue sets in, your opponent may concede a point and you claim the triumph. But before you celebrate, be certain the battle is over. After a brief armistice, the fighting might resume again — unless you can resolve the conflict so both sides are satisfied.

Write it down

. . . but rip it up. When you're angry at someone, it often helps to put it down on a piece of paper rather than yelling on the phone. But when you've finished writing, throw the letter away. A nasty note won't help solve the problem and could make things worse. Memories fade, but the written word can come back to haunt you.

The right moment

Timing is one of the most important things in life. When you have something important to say, wait for the right moment. Don't pick a time to discuss important matters with someone when they are tired or preoccupied. Be patient until the other person is relaxed and in a receptive mood. With the right timing, all things are possible!

Travel tapes

If you spend hours a day in your car, turn that travel time into a mind-expanding experience. Libraries, music and book stores have audio tapes that cover a wide range of topics. Learn financial strategies, how to find a mate or listen to the latest best-seller. Another benefit is that traffic jams and aggravating drivers won't make you angry — you've got more important things to do!

The beaks of babes

Children are like parrots. They repeat what they hear, usually at the worst possible time. When Aunt Dora visits, don't be surprised to hear something like, "My mommy says you're the fattest person in our family." As you apologize, you'll remember the lesson: If you want to keep a secret, don't tell the kids.

Gown to town

Most graduates worry about their future in the working world even as they pick up their diplomas. Fortunately, employers look for the same qualities as professors do: A thirst for knowledge, a desire to make a contribution and personal energy and enthusiasm. Cultivate these characteristics and you'll be as successful in "town" as you were in a "gown."

Secret ingredient

It's fascinating how family recipes seem to change from generation to generation, as each cook adds a little of this or removes a little of that. Using the right seasonings is a matter of choice, and the mix of ingredients varies from kitchen to kitchen. The same approach holds true in relationships. No one knows the "secret ingredient" for a successful partnership. You have to create the right recipe on your own.

Fear of intimacy

. . . may be the biggest obstacle in relationships. A new deodorant is no protection against closeness — despite what the ads say! When someone new enters your life and you begin to get close, old hurts and new fears may come to the surface. If this happens, talk to your partner — don't run away. Sharing your fears can actually help bring you closer together and create a stronger bond. Maybe intimacy isn't as scary as you thought.

QUESTIONS

Digest the question before spitting
out an answer.

— ◆ —

Unless you ask, you won't
obtain knowledge.

— ◆ —

Never answer a question with
another question.

— ◆ —

Because it's a problem — doesn't
mean there is a solution.

— ◆ —

Life is full of "whys."

— ◆ —

Yesterday's questions may be
today's answers.

Presents or presence?

Which is more important: a wonderful present or your physical presence? Let's say you flew to London to buy the finest silver platter in the world for your parents' 25th wedding anniversary. But when you return, instead of attending the party, you only send the gift. All the presents in the world won't make up for your lack of presence at this milestone event.

Being a parent

. . . is more than just a title. It takes a mature, unselfish person to help children grow into healthy adults. Too many people have children when they are still kids themselves. You must learn how to take care of yourself before you are ready to be called "mom" or "dad."

Call waiting

Juggling two phone conversations is never easy. Some people don't mind being put on hold while you answer the second line, but others consider it rude. When you use call waiting, be tactful to both parties, or be prepared to hear complaints. Don't be surprised if some people give you the busy signal in return.

Fools rush in

. . . where angels fear to tread. The chic little restaurant on the corner is for sale. You want to buy it, even though you have no experience or knowledge. Everyone warns you that most small businesses fail during the first year, but you rush ahead anyway. A few months' later, you realize your mistake, but it's too late. Sometimes wisdom comes at a very high price.

Remove the stress

. . . from happiness! Many of the happiest events in life — graduation, marriage, the birth of a child — include days of hectic preparations. As you frantically get ready for the big event, give yourself a few minutes to relax. That will let you enjoy and appreciate these once-in-a-lifetime moments. Put your worries on hold for another day — this is a time for joy!

Some good advice

Advice is only as good as the person who gives it. If you're thinking of starting a business, ask a successful entrepreneur — not a man who just filed for bankruptcy. If you want advice on raising children, ask a parent. Advice comes from a wide variety of sources. Learn who you can trust for suggestions — and who to ignore.

Marry for money

If you want to dig for gold, head for the Klondike! People who marry for money usually earn every cent. If your vision of matrimony is a gold ring surrounded by dollar signs, better change your focus. Without love, a marriage is hollow. Remember the person you go to bed with each night is the same one you'll wake up with in the morning.

Dial 911

When your life or property is in
danger, dial 911 for immediate
assistance. But don't tie up this
emergency line for routine problems.
If you need directions or you just
suffered a fender-bender, call the
police department on a regular
number. A time-saving suggestion —
program 911 into your phone, so the
push of one button can summon help
when seconds count.

COMMITMENTS

Promises are only as good as the
people who make them.

— ◆ —

Consider your priorities before
making a commitment.

— ◆ —

Too many obligations can
cause confusion.

— ◆ —

Commitment is the glue that holds
a relationship together.

— ◆ —

Before making an important
decision, sleep on it.

— ◆ —

To make a commitment, you must
understand what you are
committing to.

Life's best teacher

A young schoolboy once asked an elderly scholar, "What is life's best teacher?" Without a moment's hesitation, the scholar replied, "The mistakes you make." Therefore, it makes little sense to blame yourself for past mistakes, if you've learned valuable lessons from them. Instead, focus on the future. You have plenty of time to make mistakes in the years ahead — and to learn even more about life.

Trust your instincts

How many times have you had a gut-level feeling about a person, a place or a business opportunity? Sometimes your instincts tell you to go ahead. Other times the message is clear — avoid this situation at once. When you ignore your intuition, you can put yourself in jeopardy. Most of the time, your first reaction is correct. The secret is to stay tuned to your instincts.

Secret romances

. . . have a special allure. One of the attractions of a clandestine love affair is trying to keep things under wraps, so nobody finds out. If you believe a secret romance can add spice to your life, why not try it with your long-term partner. Enjoy a lunch-hour tryst or sneak off for a weekend getaway without the kids. You'll come back with a renewed zest for living!

Can or can't?

In most situations, the right word to use is "can." People who say, "I can't do this" or "I can't do that" always turn out to be right. That's because they give up or only go through the motions. On the other hand, if you say, "I can do that," you'll probably be right. Sometimes the only obstacle blocking your way is yourself. Turn over that stumbling block and make it a stepping stone to success.

Get-rich schemes

The only people who profit from get-rich schemes are those who sell others a dream. If you had an idea that could lead to instant wealth, would you tell other people — or keep it to yourself? Get-rich plans are sold by skilled salespeople who dangle false hopes in front of you. The only thing "fool-proof" about these schemes is that there is always a fool who believes it will work. Don't you be the fool.

Blending in

When adults remarry, children may suddenly find themselves with new brothers and sisters. It's a big adjustment for everyone. Household chores, family dinners and weekend outings may suddenly become points of contention. It's up to the parents to smooth things out and work out a daily routine that's fair to all the children. When parents present a united front, the transition goes more smoothly. With time, a blended family develops its own special flavor!

'Can't buy me love'

Money can do many things to improve your life, but it can't buy you love — or even friendship. Children learn that buying an expensive birthday present for the kid down the block won't make them best friends. But many successful adults forget this lesson from childhood and invest dollars instead of emotions.

On your mark

Get set. Stop! Rushing through life can be exhausting. When you start feeling numb at the end of the day, it's time to slow down. Being in constant motion is a poor way to experience life. If you feel like you're riding a stationary bicycle — where no matter how hard you pedal, you're getting nowhere — break the cycle of monotony. After all, your effort and hard work is designed to get you somewhere.

King of the hill

When you've climbed the ladder of life, it's tempting to relax. Learning to enjoy the finer things comes easy to most people. But it takes continued hard work to stay at the top. If you rest on yesterday's laurels, you can risk losing all your gains. Just remember — keep doing those things that made you successful in the first place.

ADVICE

Suggest, don't insist.

— ◆ —

If you give advice, know where
it's going.

— ◆ —

To make a point — talk slow and
think fast.

— ◆ —

People who need advice the most
— usually accept it the least.

— ◆ —

Remember, even experts
make mistakes.

— ◆ —

Asking for advice is not a vice.

Recycle

. . . products and people. It makes the world a better place to live. Recycling bottles, cans, jars and newspapers has become a sound habit for most people. Applying the concept to people is tougher — but even more rewarding. If you know a good friend, lover or companion for someone else, then practice recycling. One person's junk is another's antique.

Just infatuation

How do you recognize infatuation? When you see stars in their eyes! If someone is pursuing you ardently — and you're not interested — you need to send a strong, clear "no" to your admirer as soon as possible. There is nothing to be gained by leading someone on. If you have no romantic intentions, it's better to end things before they begin. That way you may be able to turn infatuation into friendship.

Stay together

If you're on a date, don't flirt with someone else, no matter what you think of your companion. If you're feeling bored, you can grin and bear it, or cut the date short. But it's unacceptable behavior to start looking for a replacement right on the spot. Leave with the same person you came with — tomorrow is another night.

You're not perfect

. . . so why do you expect perfection in others? Many people long for the perfect friend, the perfect partner or the perfect spouse, and are continually disappointed. There always seems to be a wide gap between what they are looking for and what they find. However, the only way to get "perfection" is to look it up in the dictionary.

The greatest parties

. . . end up in the kitchen. The smell of food cooking, the well-stuffed refrigerator and the comfortable table and chairs are irresistible to party-goers. If you're hosting the party, relax and enjoy the kitchen conversation. There's no use trying to keep it off limits. After all, the kitchen is the heart of the home.

Without risk

. . . there is no gain. All great accomplishments involve taking a chance. If you are venturing into uncharted waters, take your courage along. While others are saying, "I wish I had done that," or "I should have taken a chance," you can take pride in your spirit of adventure.

Where's that number?

It's frustrating when you can't find an address, a telephone or fax number after rummaging through scraps of paper. Far better to have a system for organizing and storing this crucial information. It could be a sophisticated computer database, a rolodex or simply a file of index cards in a box. All that matters is that your system works for you.

LOVE

Don't let passion throw common
sense out the window.

— ◆ —

Love doesn't necessarily
conquer all.

— ◆ —

Infatuation occurs when two
people feel they are perfect for
each other.

— ◆ —

Love me, use me, but don't abuse me.

— ◆ —

Liking yourself is just as important
as loving yourself.

— ◆ —

Love is contagious, no one is
immune and anyone can catch it.

"Shoulds"

. . . are like suitcases. The more you carry around, the more they weigh you down. "Shoulds" take the fun out of life and may hold you back. As an adult, you may still be following all those "shoulds" from your parents, without deciding whether they're right for you. In the long run, it is better to do what you "want" rather than what you "should."

About the Author

Sharon Silver, M.S.Ed., is a professional LifeStyle Educator and a respected lecturer, author, columnist, and frequent guest on national radio and television. A dynamic speaker and expert on interpersonal relationships, Ms. Silver travels throughout North America giving highly regarded lectures and workshops. She has educated and advised thousands of people on lifestyle issues in her private practice in Miami, Florida. Her last book, **Singleland: Living It, Loving It or Leaving It!** has been widely praised as a practical guidebook.

SEND US YOUR LIFELINES

Do you have any advice for others?
Suggestions for success?

Please send your **LIFELINES** to:
Sharon Silver
P.O. Box 560278
Miami, Florida 33256-0278

— ◆ —

Additional copies of
LIFELINES
by Sharon Silver,
may be ordered by sending a check
or
money order for $8.95 postpaid for
each copy to:

Distinctive Publishing Corp.
P.O. Box 17868
Plantation, FL 33318-7868
(800) 683-3722